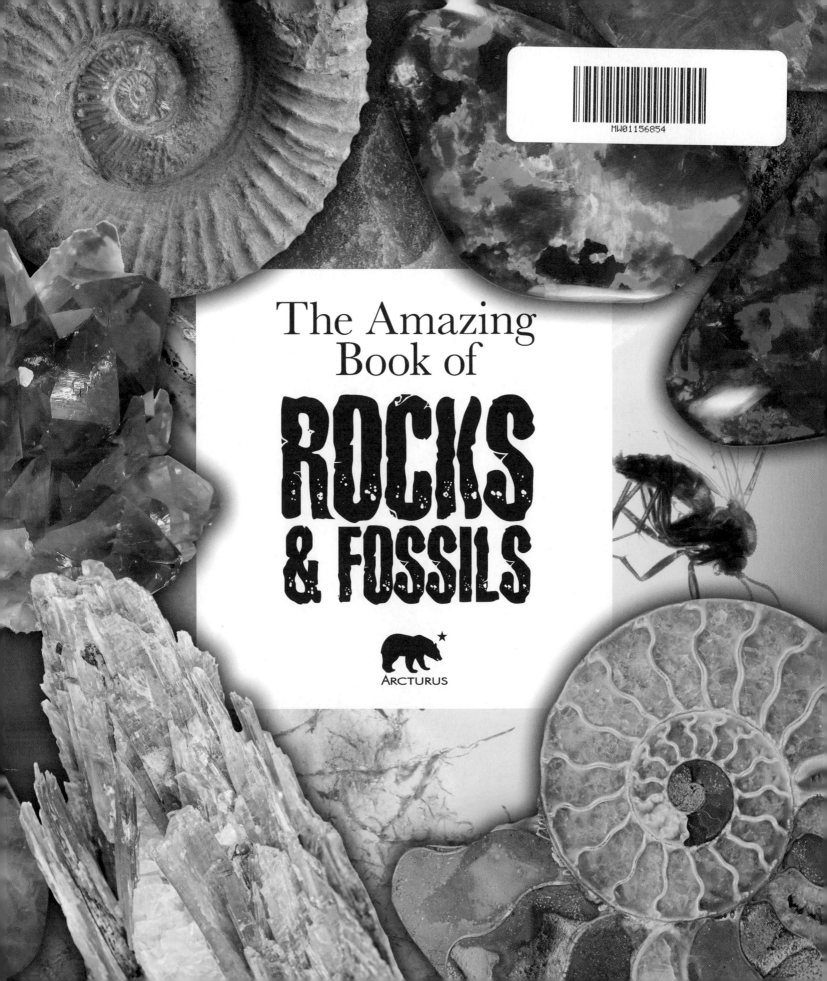

The Amazing Book of
ROCKS & FOSSILS

ARCTURUS

Picture Credits:
Key: b–bottom, t–top, c–center, l–left, r–right
Alamy Stock Photo: 18–19 (Edwin Verin), 22–23 (Peter Giovannini/imagebroker), 35tr (Artokoloro Quint Lox Limited), 36–37 (Trigger Image), 40–41 (Corbin17), 40bc (MshieldsPhotos), 42–43 (Millard H. Sharp) 16br (Luke MacGregor); **Stefano Azzalin:** 44bc; **Martin Bustamante:** 43tr, 45br; **Juan Calle:** 40br; **Mat Edwards:** 44c; **Getty Images:** 8–9 (Marco Restivo/ Moment), 14–15 (Posnov/Moment), 26–27 (Photographer/ Moment), 44–45 (James L. Amos/Corbis Documentary), 46bl (Bloomberg) ; **Kunal Kundu:** 41br; **Science Photo Library:** 4t (Richard Bizley), 4b (Mark Garlick), 10c (Spencer Sutton), 15cr (Pasquale Sorrentino), 24cr (Mikkel Juul Jensen), 26c (Gary Hincks), 28c, 30c (Gary Hincks), 36c (Jose Antonio Penas), 47c (Mauricio Anton), 47br (John Reader); **Shutterstock:** 1 (Vladimir Sazonov), 4–5 (Vadim Sadovski), 5br (Npeter), 6–7 (kurazh011), 6cl (Mariva2017), 6br (Albert Russ), 7tr (bmszealand), 8c (Designua), 8br (Ralf Lehmann), 9tr (PhotoNN), 9cr (Kletr), 10–11 (Brent 1), 10br (siamdevaa), 12–13 (Filip Fuxa), 12c (komushiru), 12br (Lisandro Luis Trarbach), 13tc (Rahayu Susilo Rini), 14c (travelview), 14br (Felix Lipov), 18br (www.sandatlas. org), 19cr (George Burba), 20–21 (l0ngtime), 20tr (travellight), 20c (tako_kr), 20br (vilax), 22c (Valeriya Pavlova), 22br (Vladislav S), 23tr (Heracles Kritikos), 24–25 (NaughtyNut), 24br (Fokin Oleg), 25tr (tommaso lizzul), 26br (Sakdinon Kadchiangsaen), 27t (Andrew Kirby), 28–29 (Peruphotart), 28br (Gavan Leary), 29br (Mr. Suttipon Yakham), 30–31 (Scott Alan Ritchie), 30br (Richard Bradford), 31tr (michal812), 32–33 (Dean Mammoser), 32c (Alessandro Colle), 32br (Davide Trolli), 33tr (Creative Idea), 34–35 (marchello74), 34c (pjhpix), 34br (vvoe), 36br (paleontologist natural), 37br (Rob Bayer), 38–39 (frantic00), 38c (psamtik), 38br (Michael Rosskothen), 39bc (MarcelClemens), 40c (gorosan), 42c (I Wei Huang), 42br (David Herraez Calzada), 42bc (Akkharat Jarusilawong), 46–47 (Juan Aunion), 47tr (JuliusKielaitis), 16–17, 16cr (Bjoern Wylezich), 17br (Vladislav Gajic) ; **Wikimedia Commons:** 11tr (NASA/JPL), 18c (Motilla), 44br (Hiroshi Nishimoto).

This edition published in 2020 by Arcturus Publishing Limited
26/27 Bickels Yard, 151–153 Bermondsey Street,
London SE1 3HA

Copyright © Arcturus Holdings Limited

All rights reserved. No part of this publication may be reproduced, stored in a retrieval system, or transmitted, in any form or by any means, electronic, mechanical, photocopying, recording or otherwise, without prior written permission in accordance with the provisions of the Copyright Act 1956 (as amended). Any person or persons who do any unauthorized act in relation to this publication may be liable to criminal prosecution and civil claims for damages

Authors: Michael Leach and Meriel Lland
Editors: Clare Hibbert and Samantha Hilton
Interior Design: Amy McSimpson and Trudi Webb
Cover Design: Stefan Holliland

ISBN: 978-1-83940-811-3
CH008249NT
Supplier 29, Date 0620, Print run 10419

Printed in China

The Amazing Book of ROCKS & FOSSILS

CONTENTS

The Earth

The Earth is a rocky ball, with a super-hot core of metal. Geology is the study of the rocks and other materials that form our planet. Geologists study how the Earth was made—and how its rocks carry on changing in amazing and beautiful ways.

Formation of the Earth

Our planet formed about 4.54 billion years ago in the cloud of gas and dust left over from the formation of the new Sun. Pulled by gravity, the gas and dust started to form clumps, which slowly grew into planets. The four planets nearest the Sun—Mercury, Venus, Earth, and Mars—formed from metal and rocky materials. The colder, outer planets—Jupiter, Saturn, Uranus, and Neptune—are mostly made of ices and gases.

At first, the super–hot Earth was molten and constantly battered by space rocks. Slowly, the Earth's surface cooled, hardening into solid rock. About 3.8 billion years ago, Earth had cooled enough for rain to fall, filling the basins that are now our oceans.

Land covers 29 percent of Earth's surface. The thick crust that forms the Earth's continents is called the continental crust.

Earth's Structure

The Earth's crust is solid rock. Beneath the crust, the mantle is made of rocks that are hot enough to partly melt and to flow very slowly. Earth's core is made mostly of the metals iron and nickel. The outer core is liquid, while the inner core is under so much pressure it is a solid ball.

1. **Crust:** Gets hotter with depth, up to 400°C (750°F)
2. **Mantle:** 500–4,000°C (900–7,200°F)
3. **Outer core:** 4,000–6,000°C (7,200–10,800°F)
4. **Inner core:** Around 6,000°C (10,800°F)

The crust beneath the oceans is called the oceanic crust. It is thinner than the continental crust, usually less than 10 km (6 miles) thick.

Around 71 percent of Earth's surface is covered by seas and oceans.

PLANET EARTH FACTS

Radius of Earth (distance from surface to middle): 6,378 km (3,963 miles)

Depth of crust: 5–70 km (3–43 miles)

Depth of mantle: Down to 2,890 km (1,796 miles)

Depth of outer core: Down to 5,160 km (3,206 miles)

Radius of inner core: Around 1,218 km (757 miles)

Earth

Rocks

Everything on Earth is made of one or more elements. Elements often combine to form natural substances called minerals. All rocks are solid mixtures of different kinds of minerals. The most common rocks are made of common minerals, which contain elements.

Grains in Granite

The common rock granite contains the minerals feldspar and quartz, with smaller amounts of mica or hornblende. These are common minerals, which all contain a number of elements including silicon, oxygen, calcium, and others.

In Torres del Paine National Park, Chile, are the peaks known as Los Cuernos ("The Horns"). This paler rock is granite.

Granite is named for its grainy texture. Large grains of the dark minerals mica and hornblende can be seen among the paler feldspar and quartz.

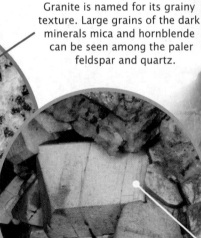

Feldspar

The mineral feldspar makes up around half of Earth's crust. Geologists call it a common "rock-forming mineral." As well as being found in granite, feldspar is in many other rocks, such as basalt, gneiss, gabbro, and diorite.

This is a chunk of feldspar, the most common mineral in Earth's crust.

MOST COMMON ROCKS IN THE CRUST

Basalt and gabbro: 43 percent

Gneiss: 21 percent

Diorite and granodiorite: 11 percent

Granite: 10 percent

Schist: 5 percent

Others: 10 percent

Zuma Rock, Nigeria, a giant chunk of gabbro

The jagged, dark summits are shale rock, which is made of hardened mud.

Most of the crust is covered by ocean, soil and plants, or cities, but rock is often exposed on high mountains and steep cliffs. These are great places to study rocks.

Volcanoes

The Earth's crust is broken into several giant pieces called tectonic plates. Volcanoes are often found where tectonic plates are moving together or apart, melting rock and forcing it to the surface. A volcano is a hole or crack in the Earth's crust which allows melted rock to escape.

Eruptions

Volcanoes are above a magma chamber, a pool of melted rock. When this magma is put under enough pressure, it rushes to the surface in an eruption, along with hot gas and ash. When it has erupted, magma is called lava. Volcanoes often grow into mountains as lava cools and hardens, building up in one eruption after another.

The volcano Mount Etna first erupted 500,000 years ago.

VOLCANO TYPES

FISSURE VENT
This is a long crack in the crust, through which lava can flow. Eruptions from fissure vents do not usually build tall mountains of cooled lava.

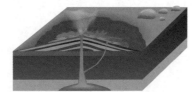

SHIELD VOLCANO
This type of volcano is named for its flattened shape, like a warrior's shield, which is made from the build-up of runny lava that flows a distance before hardening.

STRATOVOLCANO
A stratovolcano has a steep cone shape made from layers of thick lava, rocks, and ash. Eruptions are more likely to be explosive, throwing material high into the air.

MOST ACTIVE VOLCANOES

All erupting almost continually

Kilauea, Hawaiian Islands, USA: Shield volcano, 1,247 m (4,091 ft)

Mount Etna, Italy: Stratovolcano, 3,329 m (10,922 ft)

Stromboli, Italy: Stratovolcano, 924 m (3,031 ft)

Mount Yasur, Vanuatu: Stratovolcano, 361 m (1,184 ft)

Sangay, Ecuador: Stratovolcano, 5,300 m (17,400 ft)

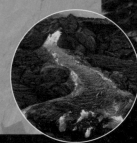

Active, Dormant, and Extinct

A volcano that is likely to erupt at some point is called "active." A volcano that has not erupted in a very long time is "dormant." An "extinct" volcano no longer has a supply of magma beneath it, so it cannot erupt again.

1. Mount Fuji, in Japan, is a stratovolcano. It has not erupted since 1707, but geologists do not agree on whether to call it active or dormant.

2. Piton de la Fournaise, on Réunion Island in the Indian Ocean, is a highly active shield volcano.

Although Etna erupts frequently, only 77 people are known to have been killed since 1500 BCE. The volcano's lava flows quite slowly, giving people time to evacuate.

Etna gets its name from the ancient Greek word *aitho*, which means "I burn."

The Rock Cycle

Earth's rocks are always changing, although they do it very slowly—over thousands or millions of years! There are three groups of rocks, each formed in a different way: igneous, sedimentary, and metamorphic. The "rock cycle" is the ways that rocks are altered or destroyed—changing from one group of rocks to another.

Rock Groups

Igneous rocks form when magma or lava cools and hardens into solid rock. Sedimentary rocks are mades when bits of rock, minerals, plants, or animal skeletons are pressed together for millions of years, slowly hardening into rock. Metamorphic rocks are formed in the crust when any rock is put under great heat or pressure, bringing about changes in its make-up. These rock-making processes are always going on, driven by the movement of Earth's tectonic plates as well as by the erosion, or wearing away, done by water, wind, and ice.

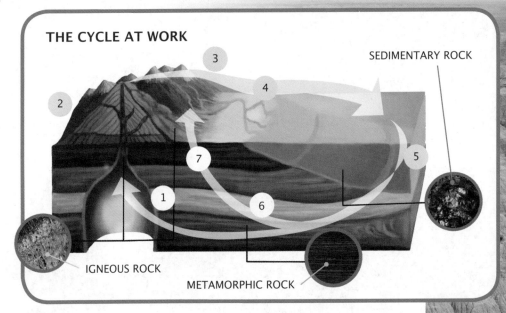

THE CYCLE AT WORK

SEDIMENTARY ROCK

IGNEOUS ROCK

METAMORPHIC ROCK

KEY

1. Rock melts into magma, then hardens into igneous rock.

2. Other magma erupts as lava from a volcano, then cools into igneous rock.

3. At the surface, rock is battered by weather and eroded.

4. Bits of rock and mineral, called sediment, are transported by rivers and rain.

5. Sediment is buried, hardening into sedimentary rock.

6. Movement of tectonic plates creates pressure and heat, forming metamorphic rock.

7. Rock is lifted to the surface by movement of the plates.

ROCK CYCLE RECORDS

Fastest tectonic plate: Tonga Plate, 24 cm (9.4 in) per year

Fastest growing mountain: Nanga Parbat, in the Himalayas, 7 mm (0.3 in) per year

Fastest eroding coast: Holderness, UK, 2 m (6.6 ft) per year

Fastest eroding mountains: Southern Alps, New Zealand, 2.5 mm (0.1 in) per year

Nanga Parbat

The Rock Cycle on Mars

Like Earth, Mars has a metal core and a rocky mantle and crust. Mars also has igneous, metamorphic, and sedimentary rocks. Mars's rock cycle is not currently very active, because it does not have moving tectonic plates and no flowing water on its surface. However, studying Mars's rocks has led scientists to think that, long ago, Mars had erupting volcanoes, flowing oceans, and falling rain.

This photograph of Mars's rocky surface was taken by the *Sojourner* rover, a robotic vehicle that explored the planet in 1997.

In Badlands National Park, USA, erosion by rivers, rain, and wind has worn the rock into buttes (isolated hills) and pinnacles (columns of rock).

The stripes are layers of different sedimentary rocks, formed at different times by volcanic ash, sand, and mud.

11

The Work of Water

Water plays a huge part in the rock cycle through weathering and erosion. Rainwater weathers, or breaks down, rock by dissolving or crumbling it. Rivers and seas carry away these fragments in a process called erosion.

Beaches

Beaches are found along coasts and other bodies of water. They are made by waves eroding cliffs, as well as coral reefs and rocks offshore. The bits of broken rock, which may be sand-sized or pebbles, are carried along and then deposited, or left behind, by waves and currents.

Over millions of years, the San Juan River, in Utah, USA, has eroded a winding canyon through the rock.

This is a sandspit, a ridge of sand stretching into the sea from a beach. It is made by waves carrying sand along the coast, then dropping it where the coastline turns a corner.

Praia do Cassino

COASTAL RECORDS

Longest beach: Praia do Cassino, Brazil, 245 km (152 miles)

Longest manmade beach: Biloxi-Gulfport, USA, 42 km (26 miles)

Longest sandspit: Arabat Spit, Ukraine, 112 km (70 miles)

Tallest sea cliffs: Kalaupapa Cliffs, Hawaii, 1,010 m (3,315 ft) high

Longest sea cave: Matanaka Cave, New Zealand, 1,500 m (4,920 ft)

Sea Caves

Caves can form in coasts because of erosion by waves. Waves are constantly wearing away cliffs, but caves are made where there is a crack or weakness in the rock, quickening the erosion in that spot.

The erosion of a cave is speeded up by rough sand and pebbles being tossed around by the waves.

Bends in a river are called meanders. They form because rivers erode rock and soil from the outer curve of their path, then deposit it on an inner curve a little downstream. This makes meanders grow larger and larger.

These very tight meanders are called goosenecks, because they are like the curved neck of a goose!

Useful Rocks

We cut rocks and minerals from the ground in open pits, or excavate them from mines dug deep into the crust. Some rocks and minerals are used as construction materials, while others find their way into factories, scientists' laboratories, farms, or artists' workshops.

Mining Minerals

Dozens of different elements and minerals are mined around the world, from glittering metals and precious gems to minerals that look dull but are extremely useful. Among the most commonly mined minerals is feldspar, which is used as an ingredient in glass, pottery, soaps, and glues. Gypsum is used as a fertilizer to feed crops, and as an ingredient in plaster and cement.

The Super Pit open-pit gold mine is in Kalgoorlie, Australia.

This halite mine is in Germany. Halite is also known as rock salt. It is used in food and to make leather, soap, printed photographs, and scientific equipment.

Ngwenya Mine

MINE RECORDS

Oldest mine: Ngwenya, Eswatini, red ochre and iron, 41,000–43,000 years old

Deepest mine: Mponeng, South Africa, gold, 4 km (2.5 miles) deep

Largest open-pit mine: Bingham Canyon, USA, copper, 4 km (2.5 miles) wide and 1.2 km (0.75 miles) deep

Most valuable mine: Cigar Lake, Canada, uranium, produces 7,850 tonnes (8,650 tons) per year

The pit is 3.5 km (2.2 miles) long, 1.5 km (0.9 miles) wide, and 700 m (2,300 ft) deep. About 28 tonnes (31 tons) of gold is dug out every year.

Discovering the Past

Rocks are a window into the past! Sedimentary rocks often form in layers, with the oldest layers at the bottom. Through studying rock layers all around the world, scientists can determine how old each layer is. This means that, when the fossil of an ancient animal or plant is found in a layer of rock, scientists can tell how long ago it lived.

Layers of rock are called strata. The study of those layers is called stratigraphy.

Rock containing flakes and chunks of gold is removed using drills and explosives, then carried away in trucks.

15

Diamonds

The mineral diamond contains only one element: carbon. A diamond is one of the hardest natural substances. In fact, the word diamond comes from the Greek word meaning "unbreakable."

Made in the Mantle

Diamonds usually form right down in the mantle, where the temperature is at least 1,000°C (1,830°F) and the pressure is very intense. The crystals grow in melted material containing carbon. They are brought closer to the surface by deep volcanic eruptions.

Most of the diamonds we have found are over 1 billion years old, but diamonds are still forming in the mantle today.

Diamonds are among the most expensive precious gemstones. Diamonds can be tinted almost any shade by impurities. The most valuable shades are blue and pink, but yellow diamonds are considered poor quality.

DIAMOND

Crystal family: Cubic

Crystal habit: Octahedral (eight-sided)

Appearance: Transparent, but may be tinted any shade

Group: Native elements

Elements: Carbon

This pink diamond is worth about US$50 million.

Diamonds are cut with many straight sides, called facets. These reflect light inside the gem, increasing its sparkliness.

Every year, people around the world spend more than US$80 billion on diamonds.

The Big Hole

Diamonds are often found in the igneous rock kimberlite, which forms in the mantle but can surge up into the crust in a vertical "pipe." Kimberlite is named after the town of Kimberley in South Africa, which is close to a diamond-rich kimberlite pipe. An open-pit mine, called the Big Hole, was dug into the pipe.

Starting in 1871, 50,000 miners used shovels to dig the Big Hole 240 m (790 ft) into the ground. They found 2,720 kg (6,000 lb) of diamonds.

Making Igneous Rocks

Igneous rock is made when melted rock cools and hardens into solid rock. Melted rock, or magma, is found in Earth's mantle and crust. The oldest igneous rocks are almost 4 billion years old, while new igneous rocks are constantly forming around active volcanoes.

Intrusive and Extrusive

There are two types of igneous rocks: intrusive (meaning "flowing inside") and extrusive (meaning "forced out"). When magma cools and hardens inside the Earth, it becomes intrusive igneous rock. If magma is forced up to the surface through a volcano, it is called lava. When lava cools down, it hardens into extrusive igneous rock.

IGNEOUS FORMATIONS

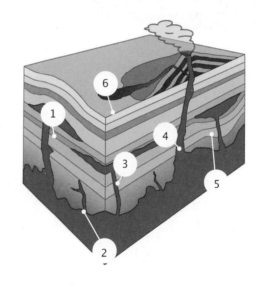

1. Magma squeezes up between layers of rock and then cools, forming a dome of intrusive igneous rock called a "laccolith."

2. Magma flows into a vertical crack, making a "dyke" of intrusive igneous rock.

3. A sheet of intrusive igneous rock is a "sill."

4. A "plug" of intrusive igneous rock is made when magma cools inside the vent of a volcano.

5. An upside-down dome is called a "lopolith."

6. Cooled lava forms extrusive igneous rock.

IGNEOUS ROCK TEXTURES

Glassy: Extrusive rocks that cooled too quickly for crystals to form
Aphanitic: Extrusive rocks with grains too small to be seen
Pyroclastic: Extrusive rocks made of fragments thrown from a volcano
Porphyritic: Intrusive or extrusive rocks with large crystals among fine grains
Phaneritic: Intrusive rocks with grains large enough to be seen with the naked eye
Pegmatitic: Intrusive rocks with massive crystals

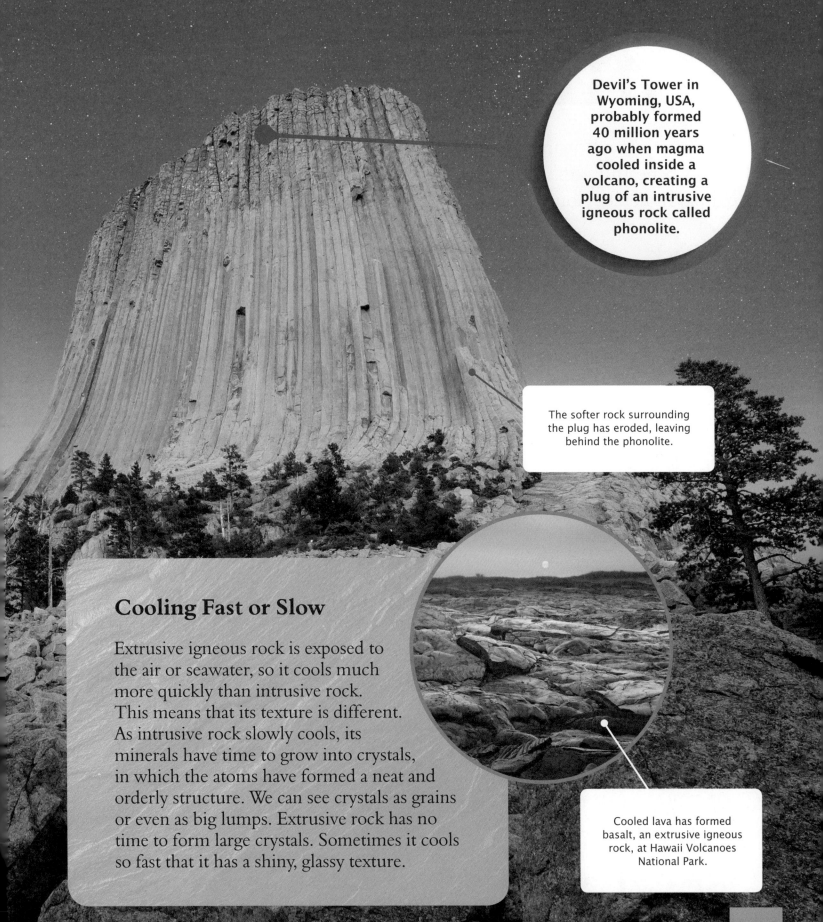

Devil's Tower in Wyoming, USA, probably formed 40 million years ago when magma cooled inside a volcano, creating a plug of an intrusive igneous rock called phonolite.

The softer rock surrounding the plug has eroded, leaving behind the phonolite.

Cooling Fast or Slow

Extrusive igneous rock is exposed to the air or seawater, so it cools much more quickly than intrusive rock. This means that its texture is different. As intrusive rock slowly cools, its minerals have time to grow into crystals, in which the atoms have formed a neat and orderly structure. We can see crystals as grains or even as big lumps. Extrusive rock has no time to form large crystals. Sometimes it cools so fast that it has a shiny, glassy texture.

Cooled lava has formed basalt, an extrusive igneous rock, at Hawaii Volcanoes National Park.

Granite

Granite is a very common intrusive igneous rock. It is formed as magma cools slowly beneath Earth's surface, growing large grains of pale quartz and feldspar minerals, alongside speckles of darker minerals.

A Hard Rock

Granite is exposed at the Earth's surface where it has been pushed upward by plate movement and the softer, sedimentary rocks that covered it have been eroded. Granite is a very hard rock that erodes more slowly than other rocks. It often forms features called tors, which are chunks of rock that stand alone.

This tor is in Dartmoor, England. The joints in the rocks are caused by weathering and erosion.

Machu Picchu

Granite's toughness has made it useful as a construction stone for thousands of years. The Inca city of Machu Picchu, in Peru, was built in the 15th century from granite that was quarried from the surrounding mountains.

The homes, temples, and warehouses in Machu Picchu are made from carefully carved blocks of granite, fitted tightly without any mortar to stick them together.

GRANITE

Formation: Intrusive

Texture: Phaneritic

Appearance: White, pink with variations of darker grains

Properties: Hard, slow to erode, and easy to polish

Minerals: Largely quartz and feldspar, plus mica, hornblende, and others

Granite

20

The mountains of Huangshan, China, are often called the "Sea of Clouds" because they look like islands above the mist.

The granite that forms the mountains was lifted to the surface 100 million years ago, then eroded into jagged peaks by glaciers.

Pines cling to rocky ledges where they can find enough soil to take root.

Pumice

Pumice is formed when lava is thrown violently from a volcano. The frothy lava cools very rapidly, creating pumice's bubbly texture. As pumice is full of holes, it is lightweight and can even float on water.

Put to Good Use

Since pumice is lightweight, it can be used to bind together concrete and plaster for structures that need to be light, such as domes and bridges. Pumice is also abrasive, which means it rubs away other materials. The rock is used in polishes and to manufacture "stone-washed," or fashionably worn-looking, jeans. Since pumice is porous, which means it allows water to pass through, it is also used to filter dirt and germs from drinking water.

The Campo de Piedra Pómez ("Pumice Stone Field"), in Argentina, is a desert covered with a layer of pumice.

Pumice is used to rub away the hard skin on feet. These "pumice stones" have been dyed.

PUMICE

Formation: Extrusive

Texture: Pyroclastic

Appearance: Usually pale, from white to brown

Properties: Lightweight, porous, and abrasive

Minerals: Depends on the lava type, but often feldspar, augite, hornblende, and zircon

Pumice

Igneous Island

The Greek island Gyali is part of an underwater volcano and is made of the extrusive igneous rocks pumice, rhyolite, and obsidian. Gyali, which means glass in Greek, is named after its glassy obsidian. The pumice is cut from huge quarries, occupying about a quarter of the island.

The Carachi Pampa volcano is one of many in the area caused by the Nazca Plate moving under western Southern America.

Pumice from Gyali's quarries is transported around the world for use in construction.

The pumice has been eroded into strange shapes by the wind, which whips around rough flakes of pumice.

Making Sedimentary Rocks

Most sedimentary rocks form after sediments—bits of rock or the remains of living things—are deposited on the floor of oceans, seas, and lakes. Over thousands or millions of years, the sediment is buried and pressed until it hardens into rock. "Chemical" sedimentary rocks are made from particles of minerals floating in water.

The Grand Canyon, in Arizona, USA, was carved by the Colorado River within the last 5 or 6 million years.

Sorts of Sediment

Sediment can be inorganic (meaning "not from living things") or organic (meaning "from living things"). Inorganic sediment is pebbles, sand, and particles of rock and mineral that are worn away from rocks by weathering, then carried along by rivers, rain, ice, wind, or rock falls. Organic sediment includes dead plants, as well as the skeletons and shells of animals.

TURNING TO ROCK

Sediment is turned to rock through deposition and cementation.

1. **Deposition**: Inorganic or organic particles are deposited, or dropped, at the bottom of bodies of water.

2. **Cementation**: Sediment slowly hardens as it is pressed beneath layers of new sediment. Minerals in the water bridge the gaps between grains of sediment, sticking them together like cement.

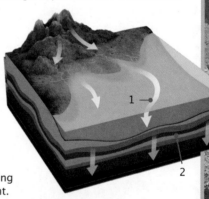

SEDIMENTARY ROCK TYPES

Clastic: Formed from inorganic sediment from weathered rocks, with separate grains and pebbles usually visible, and occasional fossils

Organic: Formed from the remains of plants and animals, with fossils and shell fragments sometimes visible

Chemical: Formed from the build-up of minerals dissolved in water, often with a texture of interlocking crystals

Siltstone, a clastic rock with fine grains

Chemical Rocks

Chemical sedimentary rocks form when water has lots of tiny particles of minerals floating around (or dissolved) in it. The mineral molecules start to join together, slowly forming rocks. This can happen quite quickly when the water is evaporating, or turning to gas, leaving the mineral molecules behind.

These "desert roses" are chemical rocks made from sand and mineral particles that formed crystals during the evaporation of a desert pool.

Many of the rock layers formed when the region was covered by a shallow sea, but over time the area has also been a beach and a swamp.

Layers of different sedimentary rocks, including sandstone, shale, and limestone, were formed by different sediments deposited here over millions of years.

Limestone

In China, the Guilin region is known for its limestone karst landscape.

Most limestones are organic sedimentary rocks that form from the build-up of shells and coral skeletons in the ocean. These animals built their shells and skeletons with the mineral calcite, which is the main ingredient in limestone. It mostly forms in clear, warm, shallow waters.

Dissolving Away

When limestone comes into contact with rainwater, which is slightly acidic, it slowly dissolves. This means that particles of limestone float away with the water. Over time, this can erode extraordinary features, such as gorges and caves. Landscapes that have been eroded in this way are called karst landscapes.

KARST LANDSCAPES

1. A stream seeps into cracks, eroding a sinkhole.

2. Rainwater soaks into the ground, eroding caves

3. Limestone pavements can form at the surface.

LIMESTONE

Formation: Organic

Texture: From tiny grains to bits of shell

Appearance: Pale, from white to light brown

Properties: Hard, dissolves in rainwater, may contain fossils

Minerals: Calcite and aragonite

Limestone

Slabs of Stone

Sometimes rain can erode limestone until it looks like slabs of stone on a paved path. This happens where a layer of limestone has been scraped clear of soil by a glacier that long ago melted. Joints and cracks in the limestone are eroded into wider "grikes."

The flat slabs of limestone are called "clints," which probably comes from the Old English word for cliff ("klint").

Steep towers of limestone, as tall as 300 m (980 ft), have been eroded over millions of years.

Traditional fishermen use trained cormorants to dive into the Li River to catch fish.

Coal

This valuable rock is made from dead plants, a process that takes millions of years. Coal is called a fossil fuel because it is made from ancient living things—and because it can be burned to produce heat and power.

Buried Energy

The ancient plants that made coal contained energy. They had made it by photosynthesis, the process through which green plants change light energy from the Sun into food energy so they can live. When the plants died, the conditions were just right to prevent the energy from disappearing: it was stored in the coal. We can release the energy by burning coal.

Problems with Coal

One of the problems with coal is that, since it takes millions of years to form, our supplies of the rock will run out within the next century. Another problem is that when coal is burned it releases the gas carbon dioxide. This traps the Sun's heat in Earth's atmosphere and is contributing to global warming.

To mine coal deep underground, shafts are dug down to the seam, then slicing and boring machines tunnel into the rock.

MAKING COAL

1. The process that formed today's coal began 360–300 million years ago, when dead plants sank into a swamp.

2. The decaying plants were covered by sediment.

3. They were pressed and heated.

4. A layer, or "seam," of coal was made.

Seams of coal are usually deep underground, but sometimes one is pushed close to the surface by plate movements.

Although machinery has made mining much less dangerous than in the past, roof collapses and explosions still put miners' lives at risk.

COAL

Formation: Organic

Texture: From fine grains to plant flakes

Appearance: Black to dark brown

Properties: Can be burned to produce heat, which can be used in power stations to make electricity

Minerals: The element carbon, plus minerals including quartz

Coal

Making Metamorphic Rocks

Metamorphic means "changed in form." Metamorphic rocks are made when any type of rock is changed by great heat or pressure. The resulting rock depends on what sort of rock it was before (called the "parent rock")—and what processes brought about the changes in its make-up and texture.

The Black Canyon of the Gunnison is in Colorado, USA.

Contact Metamorphism

There are two main types of metamorphism: contact and regional. Contact metamorphism is when hot magma leaks into solid rock. The surrounding rock is cooked by the heat, but not melted! If the rock melted, it would cool into igneous rock.

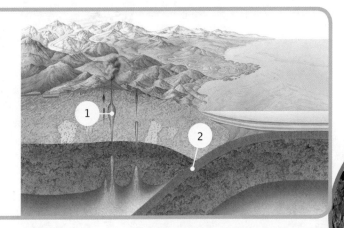

HOW METAMORPHISM HAPPENS

1. **Contact metamorphism:** Magma intrusions heat the surrounding rocks. The closer the rock is to the source of heat, the more it changes.

2. **Regional metamorphism:** The rock is pressed, twisted, and heated by plate movement.

Regional Metamorphism

Regional metamorphism happens over a wider area, or region, than contact metamorphism. Sometimes it happens just because rock is buried deep in the Earth. It is changed by the immense heat and the pressure of all the rock on top. Sometimes it is caused by the movement of tectonic plates, crushing or stretching the rock.

This metamorphic gneiss rock, in Lewis, Scotland, has been pressed so hard that it has folded like a crumpled tissue!

METAMORPHIC ROCK TEXTURES

Foliated: Sheet-like layers (caused by pressure from one side, pushing the mineral crystals into line with each other)

Banded: Layered in different shades (caused by intense sideways pressure, making the crystals line up and sort into types)

Non-foliated: Not layered (caused by being under equal pressure from all sides)

Phyllite, a foliated rock

The streaks of paler rock are dykes of pegmatite, an igneous rock.

The canyon walls are gneiss and schist, which were formed by regional metamorphism about 1.7 billion years ago.

31

Marble

When limestone is metamorphosed, it becomes marble. Pure limestone turns into white marble. When marble has black, pink, blue, yellow, or green swirls, they were created by impurities in the parent rock, such as bits of clay, sand, iron, or magnesium.

The Taj Mahal, in Agra, India, was ordered in 1632 by the emperor Shah Jahan as a tomb for his most beloved wife.

Changing Limestone

Marble is usually made where two tectonic plates are moving toward each other, crushing a layer of limestone. Sometimes, marble is made by contact metamorphism, when limestone is heated by nearby magma. During metamorphism, the calcite crystals in the limestone grow larger and lock together.

When marble forms, it is often over a wide area and extending far underground. It is carved from the ground in large quarries, such as those at Carrara, Italy.

David

Between 1501 and 1504, the Italian artist Michelangelo carved a block of marble, cut from the quarries at Carrara, into one of the world's most famous sculptures: *David*. Marble is often chosen by sculptors because it is fairly soft and easy to carve but can be polished until smooth. Michelangelo was able to show David's muscles, curls, and expression in fine detail.

In the Bible, David was a young shepherd who found fame by killing the giant Goliath.

MARBLE

Formation: Usually regional, sometimes contact metamorphism

Texture: Non-foliated with interlocking crystals

Appearance: White, but impurities create swirls in many shades

Properties: Quite soft, easy to carve, and becomes shiny when polished

Minerals: Usually calcite, plus clay minerals, mica, pyrite, quartz, and graphite

Marble

The onion-shaped dome, which bulges at its base, is 35 m (115 ft) high.

A team of 1,000 elephants hauled the marble blocks from quarries 360 km (220 miles) away.

Soapstone

This rock is so soft it feels like soap! It contains the soft mineral talc, which is used as talcum powder. Soapstone is formed by regional metamorphism from rocks such as dunite, or where super-heated groundwater flows into rock, soaking and baking it.

Softly, Softly

Soapstone's softness makes it easy to carve. It has been used for sculptures and ornaments since the Stone Age. A useful property of soapstone bowls was soon discovered: the rock absorbs heat, then radiates (or releases it) slowly, keeping food warm. When craftspeople learned to work with metal, soapstone was made into moulds to shape knives and spearheads from molten metal.

Begun in the 12th century, the Chennakeshava Temple, in India, is decorated with soapstone carvings of Hindu gods, dancers, musicians, and animals.

SOAPSTONE

Formation: Regional metamorphism or metasomatism (altered by hot water)

Texture: Non-foliated with fine grains

Appearance: Brown, greenish, or bluish shades

Properties: Very soft, easy to carve, and radiates heat slowly

Minerals: Talc, plus chlorite, mica, and others

Soapstone

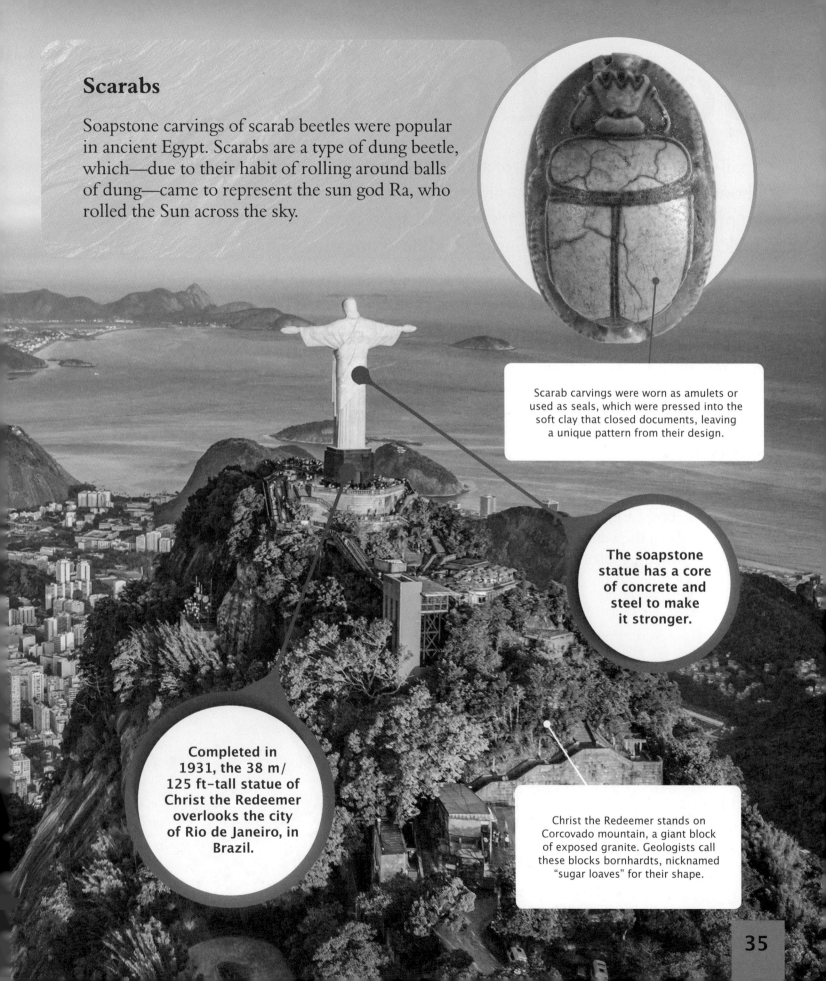

Scarabs

Soapstone carvings of scarab beetles were popular in ancient Egypt. Scarabs are a type of dung beetle, which—due to their habit of rolling around balls of dung—came to represent the sun god Ra, who rolled the Sun across the sky.

Scarab carvings were worn as amulets or used as seals, which were pressed into the soft clay that closed documents, leaving a unique pattern from their design.

The soapstone statue has a core of concrete and steel to make it stronger.

Completed in 1931, the 38 m/ 125 ft-tall statue of Christ the Redeemer overlooks the city of Rio de Janeiro, in Brazil.

Christ the Redeemer stands on Corcovado mountain, a giant block of exposed granite. Geologists call these blocks bornhardts, nicknamed "sugar loaves" for their shape.

Body Fossils

A fossil is the preserved remains of an animal or plant from thousands or millions of years ago. A "body fossil" is animal or plant parts that have been preserved in rock. Sometimes, the body parts themselves have turned to rock, but sometimes we find just an outline or an animal-shaped hole.

How Fossils Are Made

Normally, when an animal or plant dies, it rots away. However, if its body is quickly covered with sand or mud, it can be fossilized. Soft parts, such as flesh, usually rot—leaving bone, teeth, and shell. The sediment around the body slowly hardens into rock. Groundwater seeps into the body and dissolves it, but minerals in the water can fill the space, forming a rock copy.

DINOSAUR TO FOSSIL

1. A *Stegosaurus* dies on the bank of a river.

2. The body is quickly covered by sediment.

3. Body parts are slowly replaced by minerals.

4. The fossil is exposed and studied.

Studying the Past

Paleontologists are scientists who study fossils. Since all living things have evolved, or changed, over millions of years, fossils tell us what animal and plant species looked like long ago. A species is a group of living things that look similar and can breed with each other. Humans and goldfish are both species.

Paleontologists are good at finding fossils, often in sedimentary rock. They carefully dig them up, photographing and numbering every tiny piece.

This is the fossil of a nothosaur, a reptile that swam in the oceans between 250 and 200 million years ago.

The nothosaur powered through the water with its webbed feet. The skin and muscles of the feet rotted away, but the bones have been preserved.

Scientists have used robots to model how nothosaurs moved. The tail probably helped the reptile to steer.

FOSSIL RECORDS

Oldest fossil: Fossilized stromatolites (rocky mounds built by bacteria), 3.7 billion years old

Largest animal fossil: The dinosaur *Argentinosaurus*, 39.7 m (130 ft) long and 7 m (23 ft) tall, which would have weighed 70 tonnes (77 tons) when alive

Smallest animal fossil: 50-million-year-old mite on a fossilized spider, 0.17 mm (4 millionths of an inch)

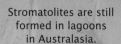

Stromatolites are still formed in lagoons in Australasia.

Sea Creatures

Studying the fossils in different layers and ages of rock has allowed scientists to work out when and where life on Earth began. Simple, tiny life forms appeared in the oceans a little over 4 billion years ago. For the next 3.6 billion years, the oceans remained the only home for all Earth's animals.

Fish

Fish are animals without limbs (arms and legs) that breathe by taking oxygen from the water through their gills. Fossils show us that the earliest fish evolved around 530 million years ago. They did not have jaws for biting, so they sucked up tiny creatures instead.

The outline of this ichthyosaur's skin has been preserved, showing it had a dorsal fin to help it steer.

Around 450 million years ago, the first fish with jaws evolved. Fossils show us their bones, spiny fins, and scales.

SEA CREATURE RECORDS

Largest extinct sea reptile: A Shastasaurid ichthyosaur, 206 million years ago, 26 m (85 ft) long

Largest living sea reptile: Saltwater crocodile, 5.5 m (18 ft) long

Largest extinct fish: *Megalodon* shark, 20–2.6 million years ago, 18 m (59 ft) long

Largest living fish: Whale shark, 12.65 m (41.5 ft)

Ichthyosaur

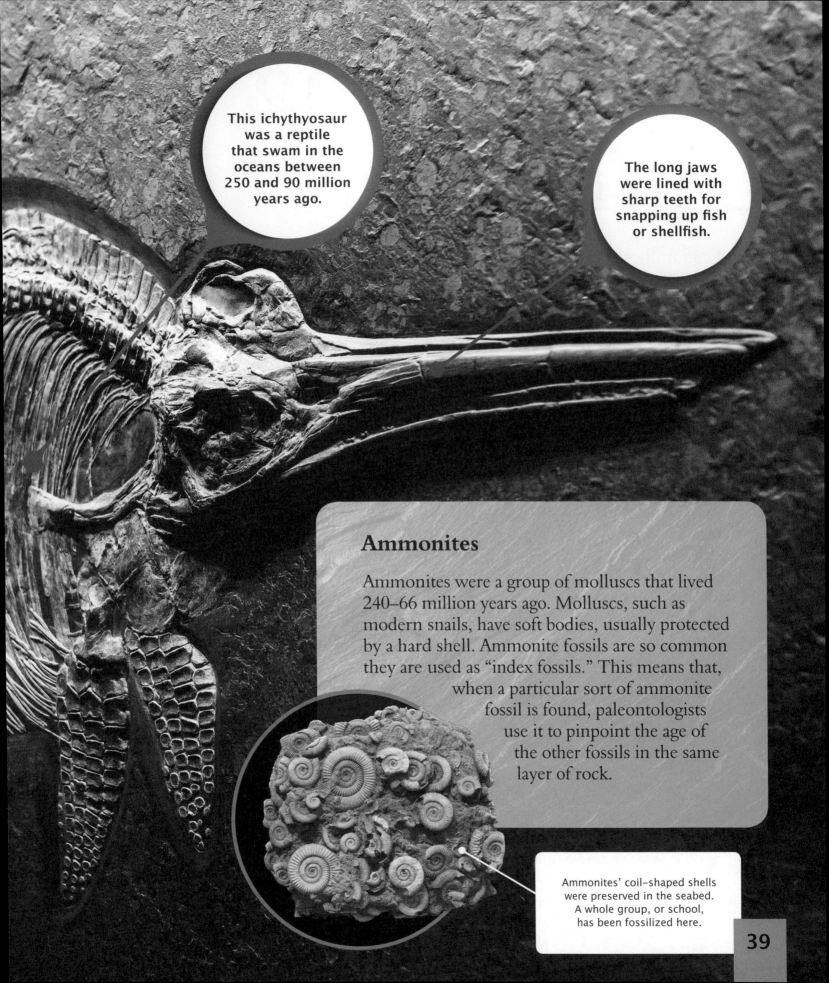

This ichythyosaur was a reptile that swam in the oceans between 250 and 90 million years ago.

The long jaws were lined with sharp teeth for snapping up fish or shellfish.

Ammonites

Ammonites were a group of molluscs that lived 240–66 million years ago. Molluscs, such as modern snails, have soft bodies, usually protected by a hard shell. Ammonite fossils are so common they are used as "index fossils." This means that, when a particular sort of ammonite fossil is found, paleontologists use it to pinpoint the age of the other fossils in the same layer of rock.

Ammonites' coil-shaped shells were preserved in the seabed. A whole group, or school, has been fossilized here.

Meat-Eating Dinosaurs

Around 235 million years ago, a special group of reptiles evolved: the dinosaurs. Around two-thirds of known dinosaurs were plant-eaters (or herbivores), while the rest were meat-eaters (or carnivores). Carnivores had strong jaws, sharp teeth and claws, and ran on their long back legs.

Fossil Clues

Studying fossilized dinosaur bones has revealed how dinosaurs were different from other ancient and modern reptiles. They walked with their legs directly beneath their body, rather than sprawled out to the sides. This helped them to breathe better and move faster.

Fossilized dinosaur eggs tell us that dinosaurs, like most reptiles and birds, made nests for their eggs.

Velociraptor Finds

The first *Velociraptor* fossil was found in 1923. *Velociraptor* was a carnivore that lived 85–70 million years ago. It belonged to the group of theropod dinosaurs, which had hollow, light bones, three-toed feet, and ran fast on their back legs. In 2007, a fossil find revealed that *Velociraptor* had feathers.

This fossilized skeleton (left) of *Velociraptor mongoliensis* was found in Mongolia, also the home of the herbivore *Protoceratops*, which is shown here winning a battle.

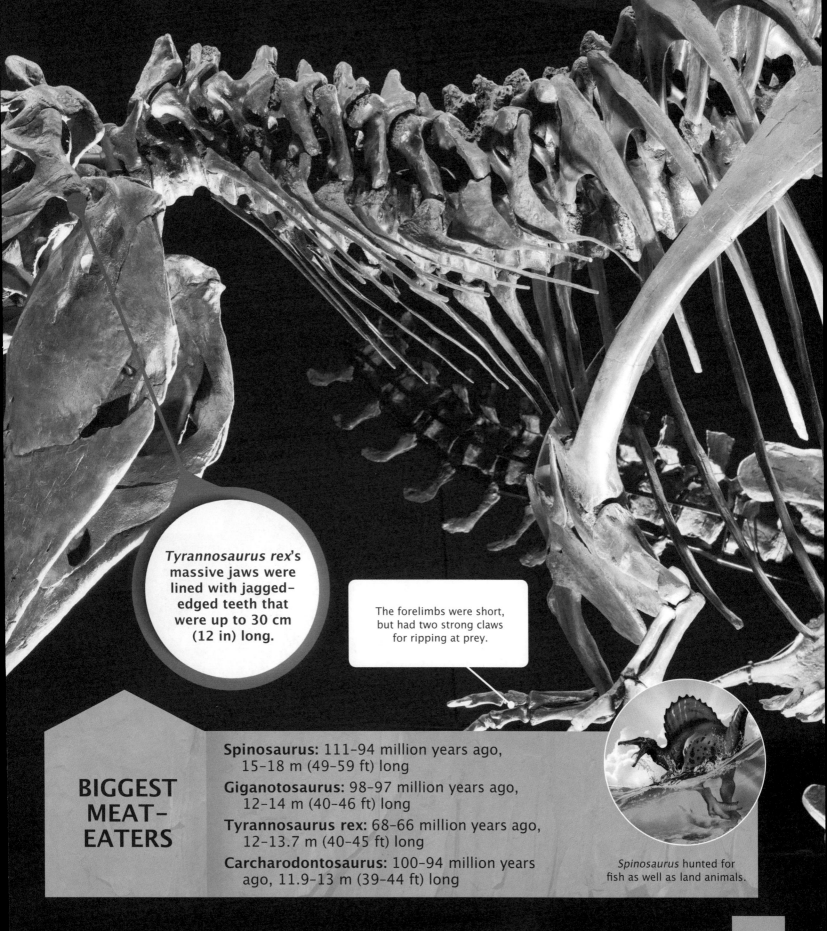

Tyrannosaurus rex's massive jaws were lined with jagged-edged teeth that were up to 30 cm (12 in) long.

The forelimbs were short, but had two strong claws for ripping at prey.

BIGGEST MEAT-EATERS

Spinosaurus: 111-94 million years ago, 15-18 m (49-59 ft) long

Giganotosaurus: 98-97 million years ago, 12-14 m (40-46 ft) long

Tyrannosaurus rex: 68-66 million years ago, 12-13.7 m (40-45 ft) long

Carcharodontosaurus: 100-94 million years ago, 11.9-13 m (39-44 ft) long

Spinosaurus hunted for fish as well as land animals.

Plant-Eating Dinosaurs

The earliest dinosaurs were all carnivores that walked on their back legs. Later, plant-eaters appeared, with some species evolving to walk on four legs to better support their weight. Some herbivores developed thick plates, horns, and spikes for protection.

Stegosaurus

Stegosaurus was a plant-eater that lived 155–150 million years ago. This tough dinosaur had a spiked tail for defending itself, and plates along its back, which may have been used for attracting a mate. More than 80 Stegosaurus fossils have been found in North America and Portugal.

This skeleton, in London's Natural History Museum, is the most complete *Stegosaurus* fossil ever found.

Skulls

Dinosaur skulls can tell us about their lives. Ceratopsids, including Triceratops, had sharp horns. These were probably used to fight off predators, but may also have been a way to attract a mate.

Paleontologists are not sure whether *Pachycephalosaurus* head–butted predators or other members of its herd.

Triceratops had three horns and a bony neck frill. The frill may have been for showing off to other dinosaurs in the herd.

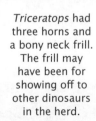

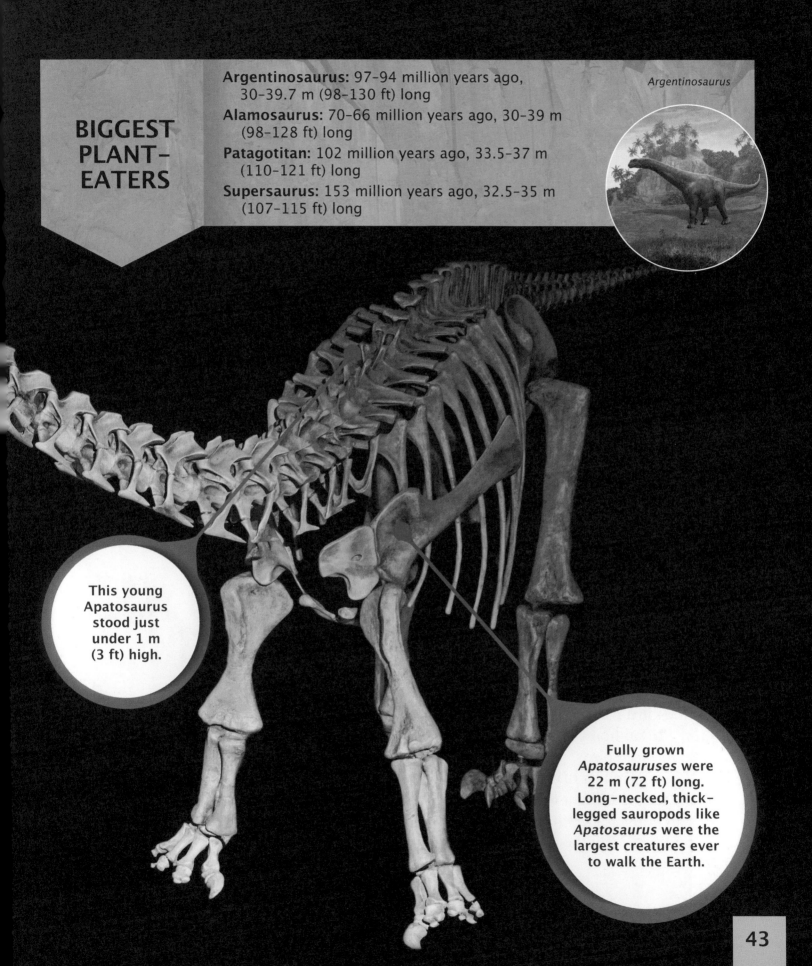

BIGGEST PLANT-EATERS

Argentinosaurus: 97–94 million years ago, 30–39.7 m (98–130 ft) long

Alamosaurus: 70–66 million years ago, 30–39 m (98–128 ft) long

Patagotitan: 102 million years ago, 33.5–37 m (110–121 ft) long

Supersaurus: 153 million years ago, 32.5–35 m (107–115 ft) long

Argentinosaurus

This young *Apatosaurus* stood just under 1 m (3 ft) high.

Fully grown *Apatosauruses* were 22 m (72 ft) long. Long-necked, thick-legged sauropods like *Apatosaurus* were the largest creatures ever to walk the Earth.

Early Birds

Most dinosaurs died out 66 million years ago, when a meteorite hit the Earth, filling the skies with dust—which blocked out the Sun, killing many plants, plant-eaters, and the meat-eaters that fed on them. Some dinosaurs survived: those that had evolved into birds. Dinosaurs are fluttering outside your window today!

From Limbs to Wings

Over millions of years, a group of light-boned, feathered theropod dinosaurs (see page 94) became smaller and more birdlike. Slowly, the bones of their front limbs changed shape to become wings, with skin flaps and powerful muscles. By 150 million years ago, the dino-bird *Archaeopteryx* was flapping its wings. *Archaeopteryx*, which means "old wing" in ancient Greek, was a halfway point between feathered dinosaurs and modern birds.

Archaeopteryx could not fly well. It probably made short bursts of flight, like modern ground-living birds such as pheasants.

MICRORAPTOR FOSSIL

Microraptor

The dino-bird *Microraptor* lived around 120 million years ago. Unlike modern birds, it had four wings! Fossils tell us that each wing was covered with flight feathers, which are longer and stiffer, giving extra power to help the creature stay in the air.

To find out more about its diet, scientists analyzed fossils of Microraptor. (above). This told them that it ate small birds, lizards, and also fish.

44

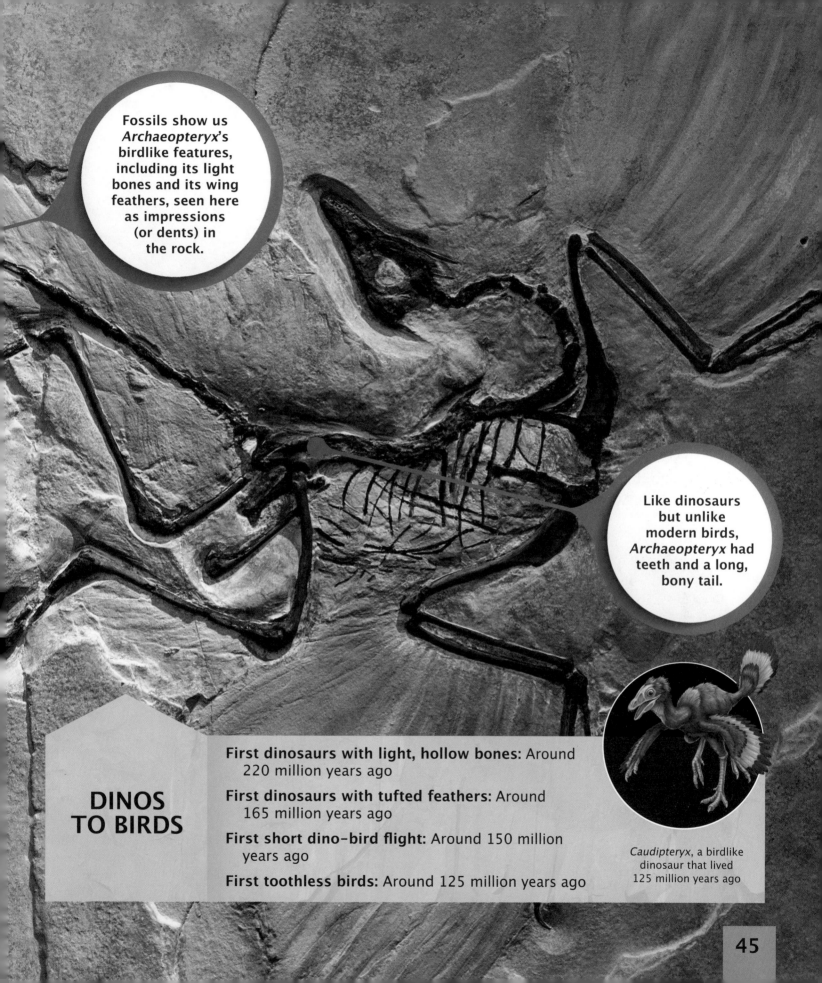

Fossils show us *Archaeopteryx*'s birdlike features, including its light bones and its wing feathers, seen here as impressions (or dents) in the rock.

Like dinosaurs but unlike modern birds, *Archaeopteryx* had teeth and a long, bony tail.

DINOS TO BIRDS

First dinosaurs with light, hollow bones: Around 220 million years ago

First dinosaurs with tufted feathers: Around 165 million years ago

First short dino–bird flight: Around 150 million years ago

First toothless birds: Around 125 million years ago

Caudipteryx, a birdlike dinosaur that lived 125 million years ago

Our Ancestors

Modern humans make up the species *Homo sapiens*, which means "wise man" in Latin. *Homo sapiens* have been around for only 315,000 years. Fossils show that our species evolved from a group of apes that lived in Africa about 7 million years ago.

Lucy

In 1974, bits of the fossilized skeleton of one of our ancestors were discovered in Ethiopia. The skeleton belonged to a female member of the species *Australopithecus afarensis*. Nicknamed "Lucy," the girl was 15 or 16 years old when she died, around 3.2 million years ago. Lucy had a small skull like an ape, but walked on two legs, like a human.

Scientists have reconstructed what they think Lucy looked like, based on the shape of her skull. Her face looked more like a chimpanzee's than a modern human's.

Lucy had strong, large jaws for chewing raw plants.

Lucy lived in a family group containing adults and children, males and females.